I Give Up

I Give Up

STUDY GUIDE | FIVE SESSIONS

LAURA STORY

WITH KEVIN AND SHERRY HARNEY

W PUBLISHING GROUP

AN IMPRINT OF THOMAS NELSON

thomasnelson.com

Published in Nashville, Tennessee, by Thomas Nelson. Thomas Nelson is a registered trademark of HarperCollins Christian Publishing, Inc.

Published in association with Creative Trust Literary Group, www.creativetrust.com, 201 Jamestown Park Dr. STE 200, Brentwood, TN 37027.

Thomas Nelson titles may be purchased in bulk for educational, business, fund-raising, or sales promotional use. For information, please e-mail SpecialMarkets@ThomasNelson.com.

Scripture quotations are taken from the Holy Bible, New International Version®, NIV®. Copyright © 1973, 1978, 1984, 2011 by Biblica, Inc.® Used by permission of Zondervan. All rights reserved worldwide. www.Zondervan.com. The "NIV" and "New International Version" are trademarks registered in the United States Patent and Trademark Office by Biblica, Inc.®

ISBN 978-0-310-103875 (softcover)

ISBN 978-0-310-103882 (ebook)

First Printing June 2019 / Printed in the United States of America

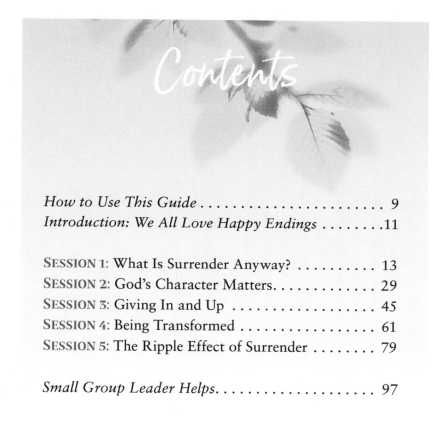

Contents

Of Note

The quotations interspersed throughout this study guide and the Between Sessions materials are from the book _I Give Up_ and the video curriculum _I Give Up_ by Laura Story. All other resources, including the small group questions and session introductions, have been written by Kevin and Sherry Harney in collaboration with Laura Story.

How to Use This Guide

The *I Give Up* video study is designed to be experienced in a group setting such as a Bible study, Sunday school class, or any small group gathering. Each session begins with a brief "talk about it" question to get you and the group engaged and thinking about the topic. You will then watch the video with Laura Story and jump into some directed small-group Bible study and discussion questions. Even though there are many questions available for your small group, don't feel that you have to use them all. Your leader will focus on the ones that resonate most with your group and guide you from there.

Each person in the group should have his or her own study guide, which includes video notes, small-group discussion questions, and daily personal studies to deepen learning between sessions. Participants are also strongly encouraged to have a copy of the *I Give Up* book. Reading the book alongside the curriculum provides even deeper insights that make the journey richer and more meaningful.

If you want to get the most out of your experience, you need to keep a couple of things in mind. First, note that the real growth in this study will happen during your small-group time. This is where you will process the content of Laura's message, ask questions, and learn from others as you listen to what God is doing in their lives. For this reason, it is important to be committed to the group and attend each session so you can build trust and rapport with the other members of your group.

Second, resist the temptation to "fix" a problem someone might be having or to correct his or her theology. That's not what this time is for. In addition, make sure you keep everything your group shares confidential. All this will foster a rewarding sense of community in your small group and give God's Spirit some space to heal, challenge, and engineer life transformation.

Following your group time, you can maximize the impact of the course with additional study between the sessions. For each session, you may wish to complete the personal study all in one sitting or to spread it out over a few days. Note that if you are unable to finish (or even start!) your between-sessions personal study, still attend the group study video session. We are all busy, and life happens. You are still wanted and welcome at the group even if you don't have your "homework" done.

We All Love Happy Endings

From our youngest days we love stories. Even if we don't think about it consciously, we each have a sense of the story arc. If the story begins, "Once upon a time," we expect it to end with the words, "And they lived happily ever after." Stories that end in victory inspire us and capture our hearts and imaginations.

Most of are not drawn to books, movies, or stories that are sure to end in defeat or disaster. We are not drawn to a narrative that focuses on surrender. We want epic victory. We celebrate winning.

When it comes to the story of Jesus, we all know it ends in a story of victory and overcoming—but that isn't the way his story begins. The path to his victory was marked by surrender, suffering, and loss. In the beginning of the Jesus' earthly ministry everyone knew that being a Christian demanded these same things. Jesus made this clear when he called people to become his followers.

> *Then he said to them all: "Whoever wants to be my disciple must deny themselves and take up their cross daily and follow me. For whoever wants to save their life will lose it, but whoever loses their life for me will save it."*
>
> **LUKE 9:23–24 NIV**

Think about the vision Jesus placed before common fishermen, tax collectors, farmers, and people from every walk of life. Be ready to deny yourself! Prepare to take up a cross . . . the tool of execution used in the Roman empire in the time of Jesus. Follow my will and plan, not your own. Be willing to lose your life. Wow! This sounds like a call to radical surrender.

These days there are many renditions of what people think following Jesus looks like. Some people see him as the one who promises to meet all of their earthly needs, fulfill their dreams, and assure them of painless days filled with endless delight.

But the call of Jesus has not changed. To be his follower is to pray, "Your will be done," as Jesus taught. To walk in maturity as a Christian is to echo the words of John the Baptist, "He must increase, I must decrease." Being a Jesus follower still means taking up his cross daily as we deny ourselves for the sake of saying yes to Jesus and his will.

God cares about the condition of our heart and the actions in our life. What delights our heavenly Father is when we say, "I give up! I surrender! I am ready to follow God's will over my own."

What Is Surrender Anyway?

— INTRODUCTION —

Tisha is a cute baby girl. Curly jet-black hair, dimples, and a smile that lights up a room. She also has a grip like a bear trap, and when she gets hold of a toy, she won't let go. Her young vocabulary is limited, but one word she has mastered is "Mine!" Daddy and Mommy are trying to teach her to share, but she finds it much more natural to cling on to everything for herself. This skill was not taught; it seems to come naturally.

Gerrit is nine and loves soccer. His coach has explained to the whole team (and the parents) that this level of soccer is all about learning the game and *not* about keeping score. But Gerrit and the other kids on the team are good at basic math and they tally every goal in their minds.

They quietly whisper, "We are ahead by two," or "That was my third goal," and with clear disappointment, "We lost by twelve goals today!" No matter what the coach says, these kids keep score, want to win, and never wave the white flag.

Ashleigh wants to be on the homecoming court. She is not conducting a formal campaign; that would be too obvious. What she is doing is exerting all of her charm and social skills to get the other kids to like her enough to cast a vote in her direction. She is leveraging every friendship and relational connection to tip the scales in her favor and help her wear that sparkling crown at halftime during the upcoming football game.

Sure, kids act this way because they

13

are still in that formational time of life when they are learning how the world works. Once we become adults we cast aside childish ways and live with humility, gracious generosity, and natural surrender. We spontaneously and naturally serve people, put God first, and stop expecting and demanding our own way.

Right?

Wrong!

The truth is, grown up people can look just like bigger versions of Tisha, Gerrit, and Ashleigh. We want what we want. Winning still matters. We navigate ways to get the crown, end up first, and gain the praise of our peers.

Living with humility does not come naturally to any of us. Willingly putting ourselves second or third does not seem to make sense. Surrendering to God's will is a learned skill that takes a lifetime to develop. If we are honest, the idea of surrender can seem foreign, unnatural, even unattractive. At this very moment, you might even be wondering, *Why am I doing a five-session study about surrender?*

The more we take our lives and place them before God, the more we will be changed from the inside out.

—— TALK ABOUT IT ——

Tell about a time in your childhood, teenage years, or adult life when you were not willing to surrender. As you look back, how was this effort to resist surrender a good choice or poor choice?

or

What moved you to choose taking part in this study about surrender?

> We think we know what is best so we ask God to help us with **our** plans on **our** terms.

—— VIDEO TEACHING NOTES ——

As you watch the video teaching segment for this session, use the following outline to record anything that stands out to you.

An invitation to surrender

....

....

....

We like to be in control

....

....

....

....

What is surrender and why do it?

....

....

....

....

Unexpected, uninvited, and unavoidable surrender

....

....

....

....

A powerful biblical example of surrender: the apostle Paul

....

....

....

....

What is your "every situation"?

....

....

....

....

There are moments when our
careful plans are wrecked
and our detailed blueprints for the
future are tossed out the window.

—— GROUP DISCUSSION ——

Read each question and take time for group members
to give honest and thoughtful responses.

1. What comes to your mind when you hear the word *surrender*? What are some possible negative connotations and what are some possible positive meanings?

A decision to study God's
Word is an investment in your
spiritual life and an active
choice to nourish your soul.

Select volunteers to read the following passages aloud
to the group and discuss the questions with each:

ROMANS 12:1–2 NIV

Therefore, I urge you, brothers and sisters, in view of God's mercy, to offer your bodies as a living sacrifice, holy and pleasing to God—this is your true and proper worship. Do not conform to the pattern of this world, but be transformed by the renewing of your mind. Then you will be able to test and approve what God's will is—his good, pleasing and perfect will.

2. What does it mean to renew our minds so that they are not lining up with the ways of the world that are relentless and all around us? What is one way you have learned to renew, change, or reorient your thinking to line up with God's ways of thinking?

3. What are some of the things that clamor for your time and attention that keep you from reading the Bible regularly and growing deeper in your faith? What could you do to control or tame some of these things so you can spend more regular time reading God's Word and growing in faith?

EPHESIANS 2:8 NIV

For it is by grace you have been saved, through faith—and this is not from yourselves, it is the gift of God.

4. What are some of the things you surrendered, gave up, or quit when you received the grace of Jesus? This surrender was not an effort to gain God's grace by works, but a humble response to God's free gift of love, friendship, and forgiveness. How has your life been better because you surrendered one of these things?

When we let go we discover
that our plans for the
future, security, and certain
health were all a façade.

5. Tell about some of the ways you try to be in control of your life, your present, and your future. How can these attitudes and actions be dangerous for your life and faith?

....

....

....

....

6. What is the difference between asking God to bless and affirm what **we want** and humbly surrendering to **his will** for our life? Give an example of what this can look like in our lives.

....

....

....

....

We like things our way. We
like to be in control.

PHILIPPIANS 3:7-8 NIV

But whatever were gains to me I now consider loss for the sake of Christ. What is more, I consider everything a loss because of the surpassing worth of knowing Christ Jesus my Lord, for whose sake I have lost all things. I consider them garbage, that I may gain Christ.

7. Laura shared her story of uninvited, unexpected, and unavoidable surrender. Tell about a time when your plans were wrecked or your blueprints were tossed in the paper shredder. How was God present with you through this season of your life?

8. What is one area of your life where you need to surrender and let go of your will and your ways? What is the circumstance to which you are holding so tightly? What is in the center of that clenched fist? What do you struggle most to let go of?

The first step toward the Savior is always surrender.

— CLOSING PRAYER —

Spend time in your group praying in any of the following directions:

- Pray for your group members as they seek to surrender in a specific area of life that they had the courage to share with you.

- Ask the Holy Spirit to show you areas in your life where you need to surrender, give up, and bow down to God's will and ways.

- Thank God for how he has been near you (and your group members) in times of uninvited and unavoidable surrender.

- Celebrate the beautiful reality that God is on the throne. Rejoice that even when we feel desperate, fearful, or uncertain, he is in charge of the universe and all the details of our life.

When we let go we actually gain something we could never find if we hold on to what we have.

Between-Sessions Personal Study

— 1. WHAT TO SURRENDER? —

As we begin this journey of surrender, take some time to identify at least one area you feel you need to surrender to God. Block out ten to fifteen minutes and find a quiet place where you can pray, wait on God, and listen. Bring this study guide with you and also a pen or pencil for writing.

- Ask the Holy Spirit to prepare your heart to humbly receive whatever word, conviction, or challenge you might receive.

- Ask the Lord to give you a clear sense of one area you need to give up or surrender fully to his will.

- Write down, in just a few words, what you feel prompted to surrender.

Perhaps also write it on a separate piece of paper and post it on your mirror at home, the dashboard in your car, or your computer at work—wherever you'll see it on a regular basis. This will reinforce the day-to-day practice of surrender.

- Pray for courage and discipline to lay this down and surrender this area to God over the coming weeks as you walk through this learning experience.

Share this conviction with a mature Christian who knows and loves you. Ask them if they will serve you and help in your spiritual journey by doing three things:

1. Pray for you in the coming weeks, asking God to help you fully surrender in this area of your life.

2. Give you input, right now, on how they feel you could grow in surrender in this specific aspect of your life.

3. Check in with you over the coming weeks and ask how you are doing, what you are learning, and how your life is changing as you surrender this area of life to Jesus.

— 2. LIFE INSPECTION —

Surrender begins with an honest survey of our heart, attitudes, and relationships. Find a quiet place and set aside ten to fifteen minutes. Bring a note pad and something to write with, or make a list on your phone, tablet, or computer. If you like to keep notes on a device rather than on paper, take a moment to put your device on airplane mode or disconnect your internet so you don't get beeps and vibrations that could distract you in this sacred time with God.

Begin with prayer. Ask the Holy Spirit of God to search your heart, mind, and life. Tell the Father that you desire to yield your will to his ways and surrender to all that he has for you, even if it is hard. If you like writing out your prayers, use the space provided below:

Reflect on God's Word. Read the following verses a couple of times, slowly, and make them your prayer.

Search me, God, and know my heart;
Test me and know my anxious thoughts.
See if there is any offensive way in me,
And lead me in the way everlasting.
PSALM 139:23–24 NIV

Write down two or three specific areas you believe you have not yet surrendered or need to surrender more completely to God's will for your life. Think about attitudes you need to surrender. Ponder actions or life patterns God might want you to yield to him. Let your mind run through your relational world and identify specific places you might need to surrender to another person in a way that would honor God and mature you.

Area One: I need to surrender . . .

Area Two: I need to surrender . . .

Area Three: I need to surrender . . .

Identify one action step of surrender for one of the areas above. What can you do, say, stop doing, or stop thinking and what will move you toward a more surrendered life?

My Action Goal:

....

....

....

....

3. CONFESSION IS A BIG PART OF SURRENDER

The Bible invites us to be people of confession. We are to confess our sins to God as well as to others. Read the two passages below and then take time to confess to God whatever the Spirit puts on your heart. Also, if you have wronged someone and need to confess your wrong, be sure to contact this person as soon as you can and admit where you were wrong as well as ask for their forgiveness. This is a radical and powerful act of surrender.

If we confess our sins, he is faithful and just and will forgive us our sins and purify us from all unrighteousness.

1 JOHN 1:9 NIV

Therefore confess your sins to each other and pray for each other so that you may be healed.

JAMES 5:16 NIV

4. KEEP A SIMPLE JOURNAL OF LESSONS

Use the journaling space below to note what the Holy Spirit is stirring within you that you may not have been aware of before or an area you hadn't quite considered needing to surrender.

5. REFLECT

Use the space provided below to write some reflections on the following topics:

- How can reading the Bible regularly, and seeking to follow what God teaches you through his Word, help you grow in surrendering to his will and move you away from seeking (or demanding) your way so often?

The more we are exposed to God's Word and submit our lives to his teaching, the more we are changed into his likeness.

- What makes you afraid to surrender all of your life, the big stuff: your future, your dreams, and especially your plans to God?

- Do you find it more difficult to surrender the "big stuff" or the "little stuff," such as how you approach daily tasks, respond to bumps in the road, deal with setbacks or schedule changes, family, work etc.? Why?

....

....

....

....

....

—— RECOMMENDED READING ——

As you reflect on what God is teaching you through this session, you may want to read chapters 1 and 2 of *I Give Up* by Laura Story. You also might want to read chapters 3–6 as you get ready for the next session.

God's Character Matters

— INTRODUCTION —

On the eleventh hour of the eleventh day of the eleventh month of 1918, the German army surrendered to the Allied forces and the First World War came to an end. The Germans signed an armistice and committed to stop fighting and seek peace. All outward signs indicated that the Allied forces would win this horrific conflict. In the end, Germany surrendered to their enemies . . . the very people they were seeking to conquer.

Twenty-seven years later, after six years of brutal conflict, World War II ended in 1945. The war that involved over 100 million people from more than 30 countries climaxed when the Axis powers of Germany, Italy, and Japan surrendered to the Allied forces on both Atlantic and Pacific fronts. Again, as in all wars, one group surrendered to the ones they were fighting against, their enemies.

All through history wars have raged and each one seems to end the same. Two enemies have battled and one finally gives up. They bow to the power of their enemy.

God's story is upside-down and radically different. When we surrender to the God who made us, we are bowing our knee to the one who loves us most. Yielding to the leadership of Jesus is not acquiescing to a military power that wants to conquer, but it is embracing the one who wants to lift us up and empower us. Saying, "I give up," and declaring, "Your will be done," is throwing ourselves into the arms of the God who calls us his friends!

Surrender isn't a free fall; it
is gracefully descending into
gentler, more capable hands.

—— TALK ABOUT IT ——

What is the difference between surrendering to an enemy who wants to dominate you or surrendering to a father who wants only the best for you? How is surrendering to the Father one of the wisest things you could ever do?

or

What are some of the characteristics of God that made it easy for Jesus to surrender to him?

Surrender becomes less scary
and less risky when we know
whom we are surrendering to.

— VIDEO TEACHING NOTES —

As you watch the video teaching segment for this session, use the
following outline to record anything that stands out to you.

Is surrender a daredevil free fall or a wise decision?

Joseph Williams and Timothy . . . a story of trust!

We are not called to blind and mindless surrender

Who is the God to whom we surrender?

The God who sees me

....

....

....

We don't just surrender for
surrender's sake; we surrender
to the only one capable of
handling our circumstances.

—— GROUP DISCUSSION ——

Read each question and take time for group members
to give honest and thoughtful responses.

1. What are some of the reasons we avoid or resist surrender? Why is this
   understandable?

....

....

....

....

2. Most of the things worth doing in this life have a price and demand some kind of
   surrender. Write down one or two things you have done that had a cost related to
   you doing them. Then, write down a couple of things you had to surrender to do
   each of these things.

Something valuable I have done in my life:

_____

What did I surrender to do this thing?

_____

Something valuable I have done in my life:

_____

What did I surrender to do this thing?

_____

Share one of these with your group.

3. How is surrendering to God an act of letting go (scary and mysterious) and also an act of accepting God's control and leadership (comforting and exciting)? Give an example of how you have experienced these contrasting emotions while seeking to surrender to God.

4. Laura tells the story about entrusting her son to a capable doctor. Tell about a time you trusted someone enough to surrender yourself or someone else to them. What was it about this person that gave you the peace and confidence you needed to surrender?

Leader, read Psalm 23 aloud to the group and
discuss the questions that follow.

5. What are sheep like and why do they need a good shepherd? What would happen
    to sheep if they had no shepherd or decided to run from their shepherd rather than
    follow?

    ....

    ....

    ....

    Yahweh, the King of kings and
    Lord of lords, was compared
    to a lowly shepherd.

6. What aspects of God's character do you discover in Psalm 23? How do each of
    these instill confidence and trust to surrender your life to his leading?

    ....

    ....

    ....

    ....

7. What does our culture teach us about self-sufficiency in contrast to trusting
    others? How can some of our cultural attitudes get in the way of us trusting God
    fully and consistently?

    ....

    ....

    ....

    ....

8. What does it mean to say that "God sees me"? How can a deep certainty that God sees you grow your ability to trust him and surrender to his will and ways?

    ....

    ....

    ....

    ....

9. If I trust God as the true Shepherd of my life, how should this grow my ability to trust him and surrender in one of these areas of my life? Specifically, how can your group members pray for you as you seek to grow in surrendering in one of these areas?

    *   For his **provision** for me and those I love

    *   For his **guidance** in hard times

    *   For his **power** over the fears I face

    *   For his **protection** over my life

Although surrender may be one
of the best things for us, it isn't
exactly the easiest thing to do.

35

— CLOSING PRAYER —

Spend time in your group praying in any of the following directions:

- Thank God for his character and attributes that make it possible for you to surrender to him and trust him, even in hard times.

- Ask God to help you trust him and follow him like sheep with a good shepherd.

- Ask for courage to surrender to God in areas you have never been able to fully lay all you have and are before him.

- Lift up praises for times you have surrendered to God in the past and he has proven himself loving, faithful, and trustworthy.

There is secret joy in letting go!

Between-Sessions Personal Study

1. GETTING TO KNOW MY GOOD SHEPHERD

Take time to read Psalm 23 slowly, three or four times. Meditate on each attribute or characteristic of this Good Shepherd, because it is a picture of your Lord.

Write down each attribute of God as the Good Shepherd that you identify in the spaces provided below.

After you have identified as many characteristics as you can, write down *how* this characteristic increases your trust in God and helps ease the difficulty in surrendering more to him.

The Good Shepherd is: _____.

If this is true about the Lord, my Good Shepherd, I can trust and surrender _____ to him.

The Good Shepherd is: _____.

If this is true about the Lord, my Good Shepherd, I can trust and surrender _____ to him.

The Good Shepherd is: _____.

If this is true about the Lord, my Good Shepherd, I can trust and surrender _____ to him.

The Good Shepherd is: _____.

If this is true about the Lord, my Good Shepherd, I can trust and surrender _____ to him.

The Good Shepherd is: _____.

If this is true about the Lord, my Good Shepherd, I can trust and surrender _____ to him.

Surrender takes more than
work—it takes risk!

— 2. WRITE A REFERENCE —

Imagine you were talking to a person who is not yet a follower of Jesus and they say to you, "Why should I trust God? Why would anyone choose to give up control over her own life to follow Jesus? How would God ever have a better plan for my life than what I could come up with on my own?"

Take time to write out how you would answer these questions. We don't have to rely merely on our own testimony—for when we are less than faithful, the Scripture still stands! Look up instances in Scripture where God's trustworthiness is exemplified. Look for times where people trusted in difficult or extreme circumstances, as well as in seemingly normal or daily circumstances. Use both Old and New Testaments and pay attention to the character's relationship with God (i.e.: give examples for them to read).

....

....

....

....

—— 3. WHAT IS IN A NAME? ——

In the ancient world, names meant far more than they do to most people today. A name was not just something people called you. A name was a window into a person's character, their nature, who they were.

Take time to write down ten names for God found in the Bible. This can include names for the Father, Son, or Holy Spirit. If it would be helpful, do a Google search for "Biblical names for God, biblical names for Jesus, or biblical names for the Holy Spirit."

Under each name, write down what this name teaches you about the character of God and why you should trust him more in light of this name.

Name for God: _____

What this name teaches me about God and why this name should grow my trust in God and my willingness to surrender:

_____

Name for God: _____

What this name teaches me about God and why this name should grow my trust in God and my willingness to surrender:

_____

Name for God: _____

What this name teaches me about God and why this name should grow my trust in God and my willingness to surrender:

_____

Name for God: _____

What this name teaches me about God and why this name should grow my trust in God and my willingness to surrender:

_____

Name for God: _____

What this name teaches me about God and why this name should grow my trust in God and my willingness to surrender:

_____

Name for God: _____

What this name teaches me about God and why this name should grow my trust in God and my willingness to surrender:

_____

Name for God: _____

What this name teaches me about God and why this name should grow my trust in God and my willingness to surrender:

_____

Name for God: _____

What this name teaches me about God and why this name should grow my trust in God and my willingness to surrender:

_____

Name for God: _____

What this name teaches me about God and why this name should grow my trust in God and my willingness to surrender:

_____

Name for God: _____

What this name teaches me about God and why this name should grow my trust in God and my willingness to surrender:

_____

We are called to surrender to the only one capable and able to handle whatever our circumstances really are. We are called to surrender our lives and our moments to God.

Use the journaling space below to note what God is teaching you through the exercises above.

....

....

....

....

....

—— 4. REFLECT ——

Use the space provided below to write some reflections on the following topics:

- What jumped out at me most this week about God's character as a reason I can trust God with my whole life?

- What have I learned about God that is encouraging me to want to surrender more to him?

....

....

....

....

....

—— RECOMMENDED READING ——

As you reflect on what God is teaching you through this session, you may want to read chapters 3–6 of *I Give Up* by Laura Story. You also might want to read chapters 7–9 as you get ready for the next session.

Giving In and Up

—— INTRODUCTION ——

Imagine a strange and simple experiment.

What if a person did everything in life their own way? What if her every decision was myopic and utterly self-centered? From the cradle to the grave *"My will be done!"* would be her driving mantra. In every stage of life, there would be no surrender to the will of others, no acquiescing to laws and cultural guidelines, and certainly no bowing the knee to God's commands or teaching. What might this kind of life look like?

This little girl would never learn to share . . . never! *What is mine is mine! As a matter of fact, what is yours is mine!* She would hoard, consume, and steal from others without blinking or blushing. She would demand her way in every situation and with every group of people. Imagine the quality of her friendships . . . if she had any friends at all. Think about how others

would view her. How would this approach to life shape the character of this girl?

As a teenager, she would continue to grow this lifestyle of no surrender: no humility and or cooperation with anyone else. Her every decision would be driven by what would be best for her, what made her feel good, and what she wanted at any given moment. *Me first! I matter most! My way is not only the best way, it is the only way!* It never crosses her mind to ask such questions as, "What would my friends like to do?" "How does this impact others?" or "Does this honor my parents?" At this point, consider how other teens and her parents view her. The other young people her age have formed a clear picture of who she is, and when she is not around, they articulate their feelings with piercing clarity. Most people simply try to avoid her.

The years pass, and she would love to

get married someday. The problem is, she can't seem to find a man who can meet all of her needs, focus on her alone, and understand that everything really is about her. The idea of having children seems repulsive. Kids would only demand things of her. A family would cramp her style and get in the way of her dreams. Why complicate things?

Faith in God makes no sense to her. Why believe in a deity who has a plan for her life? She already has plans of her own. Why follow a heavenly being who says no to her whims and desires? Why bow her knees, heart, and life to anyone, even a divine creator?

The sad thing is that people try this strange experiment over and over again, at varying levels of intensity. For most of us, there is a natural propensity toward a *"My will be done!"* approach to life. It is easy to be swept into a mindset that says, "What I want is the most important thing of all." But God offers a dramatically different kind of life. One that is not natural but supernatural!

There is nothing natural about surrender.

—— TALK ABOUT IT ——

What are some possible consequences we could face if we refuse to surrender but seek to do everything our own way and according to our own self-will?

or

Tell about a time you suffered a hard consequence because you demanded that things be done your way.

There are parts of us that bristle
at the idea of surrender.

— VIDEO TEACHING NOTES —

As you watch the video teaching segment for this session, use the
following outline to record anything that stands out to you.

A real-life story . . . "He took my ball!"

Surrender does not come naturally

Using God to get what I want

Not my will but yours be done. Isn't
this the essence of surrender?

Jesus' example of surrender

Jesus' relationship with the Father:

A divine partnership . . .

Awareness of the Father's power and authority . . .

Desire to follow the Father's will . . . "Not my will but yours be done . . ."

Jesus knew his Father was
not just a mighty God,
but a saving God.

⸺ GROUP DISCUSSION ⸺

Read each question and take time for group members
to give honest and thoughtful responses.

1. We all have stories of children and teens we know who demanded to do things
    their own way and learned a lesson about the consequences of refusing to
    surrender. Share one of your stories and a lesson you learned about surrender in
    the process.

    ....

    ....

    ....

    ....

2. Share honestly about something that is really hard for you to let go of or give
    up. How do you respond when someone does something that makes you have to
    surrender in this area of your life? How do you respond when God challenges you
    to surrender in this area?

    ....

    ....

    ....

    ....

There is a Latin phrase for
sin that translates: "turned or
curved inward on oneself."

Select volunteers to look up and read the following passages
aloud to the group and discuss the questions for each.

Jeremiah 17:9; Genesis 6:5; and Matthew 15:18–19 NIV

3. How can a heart turned in toward oneself and selfish desires lead to all sorts of sin? How can giving in to God's will be an antidote to the sickness of the human heart?

....

....

....

4. If we are not attentive and careful, we can actually use God to get what we want. We can twist the Bible's teaching to affirm our own selfishness, self-serving lifestyles, and desires. What are some of the ways Christians can manipulate the Bible and our faith to making it all about us? What are some of the dangers and possible consequences of this kind of "faith"?

....

....

....

Who of us has not been guilty
of using God as a means
to get what we want?

John 6:35–39; John 14:28–31; John 5:19; and Luke 22:41–44 NIV

5. What do you learn about giving in and giving up as you read these passages about Jesus? How can you follow this example in the flow of a normal day?

....

....

....

> Yet knowing his Father's love and his Father's power, there was still something Jesus was still more consumed with: his Father's will.

6. When we know the power and authority of our heavenly Father, it becomes easier to surrender to him. Tell about one of your favorite Bible stories that reveals the power and sovereign authority of God. How does this story elevate your confidence that you can trust him and surrender even when you are afraid?

....

....

....

....

2 Corinthians 1:3–7 NIV

7. How does receiving the comfort of God, and knowing the comforting nature of our heavenly Father, free you to surrender and trust him in the hard times of life? What does the apostle Paul teach us about extending and sharing the comfort of God to others and how can God use you to help others trust him more?

....

....

....

....

> None of us should be surprised
> when the road God leads us
> down is less comfortable and less
> sturdy than we expected.

8. One of the reasons we have a hard time surrendering to God is that we are holding too tightly to other things. What do you need to hold more loosely (or let go of) so that you can surrender more to God's will and way for your life? How can your group members pray for you as you seek to willingly give up this thing to God?

....

....

....

....

> We don't surrender because it's easy;
> we surrender because it's Jesus' way.

—— CLOSING PRAYER ——

Spend time in your group praying in any of the following directions:

- Pray for courage to hold the things you love with a looser grip . . . even with open hands. Ask God to give you a trusting heart that is quick to give in and give up when he is leading you.

- Confess where you have been refusing to surrender and ask for God's grace and comfort to fill you.

- Thank Jesus for giving you such a compelling and beautiful picture of a life surrendered to the Father and pray that you will be more like your Savior.

- Pray the words of John the Baptist . . . "He must increase and I must decrease!"

We will not all be asked to die in obedience to the will of God, but every one of us is called to live for it.

Between-Sessions Personal Study

— 1. I DON'T WANT TO LET GO! —

List three or four things you have a hard time letting go of and fully giving up. It could be material things, time, influence, money, control, the future, your plans, or personal relationships such as your marriage, parenting, friendships, or your social life. What are things that you have a tight grip on and really don't want to let go of?

- _____
- _____
- _____
- _____

Pick one of these areas to really focus on. Write it again in the space provided here:

- _____

Respond to the questions below:

Why is it hard to let go of this and surrender it?

....

....

....

....

Why am I holding on so tight?

....

....

....

....

What negative consequences am I experiencing now or might come my way by holding too tightly to this?

....

....

....

....

What good things might God do if I can fully and truly let this go and surrender to him?

....

....

....

....

What is one practical step I can take this week to begin loosening my grip on this?

....

....

....

....

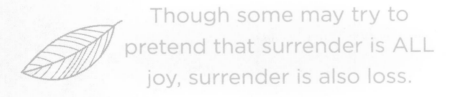

Though some may try to pretend that surrender is ALL joy, surrender is also loss.

— 2. WALK WITH JESUS —

Over the coming weeks read all four Gospels in the New Testament (Matthew, Mark, Luke, and John). In your Bible or in a journal, record each time you see an example of Jesus giving up or giving in. Pay close attention; these are beautiful moments. Then, write down what you learn about surrender from the example of Jesus.

Next, use the space below to write a composite picture of what you learn about surrender from Jesus in each of the four Gospels. Try to distill it down to a clear and impactful picture you can remember as you seek to live a surrendered life.

A Picture from the Gospel of Matthew:

....

....

....

....

A Picture from the Gospel of Mark:

....

....

....

....

A Picture from the Gospel of Luke:

....

....

....

....

....

....

A Picture from the Gospel of John:

....

....

....

....

....

....

Finally, shape these lessons into a simple list of your top three takeaways about surrender and what the example of Jesus should mean for your life:

1. _____

2. _____

3. _____

The work of surrender
is HARD WORK.

— 3. MEMORIZE SIMPLE TRUTH —

Take time to memorize these two short, simple but radically life-changing verses from the Bible:

John the Baptist declared:

> "He must become greater; I must become less."
> **JOHN 3:30** NIV

Jesus prayed to the Father:

> ". . . not my will, but yours be done."
> **LUKE 22:42** NIV

Jesus was one hundred percent
consumed with God's will.
It was the deciding factor
in any decision he made.

Keep a simple journal of what God is calling you or encouraging you to give up and give in to.

My receiving is preceded
by my letting go.

——— 4. REFLECT ———

Use the space provided below to write some reflections on the following topics:

- What I observe about myself and why I resist surrender.

- How my perspective changes when I loosen my grip and let go of things I only think I control.

- My personal experience or understanding of becoming less so that Jesus might become more.

In order to receive anything,
our hands must be empty.

——— RECOMMENDED READING ———

As you reflect on what God is teaching you through this session, you may want to read chapters 7–9 of *I Give Up* by Laura Story. You also might want to read chapter 10 as you get ready for the next session.

Being Transformed

— INTRODUCTION —

Imagine an engaged couple who are excited for their wedding day. It is just one month away and they are both looking forward to this next chapter of their life together. They know that getting married will probably mean a few adjustments to their lives, but they keep telling each other, "We will be the same people after the wedding ceremony. How much can things really change?" Then, in a conversation with a wonderful couple they respect who has been married for over three decades, they dare to ask the question, "How much will things really change after we tie the knot?"

They are both shocked as this dear couple tells them, "More than you can imagine or dream!" They go on to tell story after story about how being married for over thirty years has changed their dreams, life patterns, personal habits, schedules, and everything else ever since they said

the words, "I do!" They go on to explain that the journey of being married has been transformational, challenging, stretching, and more wonderful than they could have dreamed. The younger couple realizes they have no idea of all that will change on their wedding day just a month away.

Five exciting years later, this young couple now has a clearer picture of the significance of being married. They would say that almost everything in their lives has changed . . . in one way or another. They love being married. In five years they have both changed more than they could have dreamed. They call the same older couple and set up a lunch. They want to share some exciting news. Over lunch, they let the cat out of the bag. "We are pregnant! In six months we will be holding a baby in our arms!"

This young couple dares to ask the

question. "We know you have raised three wonderful children. Can you help us prepare for being parents? *What really changes once the baby is born?*"

If you are a parent, you already know the answer. *Everything!* More than you dream! It is glorious, wonderful, taxing, exhausting, joy-filled—and this young couple will never be the same.

Anyone who thinks that building a good marriage or raising a child will demand only a few minor adjustments to their life does not have a clear picture of what lies ahead. These moments are life altering.

Deciding to live each day surrendered to the God who made you is much the same. When we stop saying, "My will be done," and declare, "Your will be done," everything changes. It will stretch us to the limit. And we will find meaning, joy, peace, and a richness of life beyond our wildest imagination. Surrender to God changes everything . . . including us!

Surrender always requires a willingness to change.

— TALK ABOUT IT —

Think about a major life event (for example, getting married, the birth of child, being transferred to a different job, a geographic move), and share how your life changed once you made this step in your life.

or

If you have made a commitment in your life to surrender something very specific to God, or an event or circumstance has called for a significant surrendering, tell how this has changed who you are as a person.

If you are truly asking God to teach you to surrender, it is impossible for everything to stay the same!

— VIDEO TEACHING NOTES —

As you watch the video teaching segment for this session, use the following outline to record anything that stands out to you.

What changes when we surrender? We do!

Surrender transforms our character

Understanding grace leads to a new kind of living

First steps of surrender

Obstacles to living a surrendered life

Put off the old self

Put on the new self

A biblical story . . . not willing to surrender

God has something better

Surrender requires active participation.

—— GROUP DISCUSSION ——

Read each question and take time for group members
to give honest and thoughtful responses.

1. As you begin session 4 of this study, share what opportunities of surrender have
    come up (think back over the past weeks since first praying the initial prayer of *I
    Give Up*)?

    ....

    ....

    ....

    ....

2. As you have been learning to surrender to God's will as a life practice, where
    have you noticed joy in your heart and life? In what ways does living more of a
    surrendered life help you feel more connected to God?

    ....

    ....

    ....

    ....

Select volunteers to read the following passages aloud
to the group and discuss the questions for each:

EPHESIANS 4:1–3 NIV

As a prisoner for the Lord, then, I urge you to live a life worthy of
the calling you have received. Be completely humble and gentle; be
patient, bearing with one another in love. Make every effort to keep
the unity of the Spirit through the bond of peace.

3. What are some of the ways our character changes and matures when we live a surrendered life? What character growth might we miss if we resist surrender?

Surrender should affect our character.

EPHESIANS 2:1–6 NIV

As for you, you were dead in your transgressions and sins, in which you used to live when you followed the ways of this world and of the ruler of the kingdom of the air, the spirit who is now at work in those who are disobedient. All of us also lived among them at one time, gratifying the cravings of our flesh and following its desires and thoughts. Like the rest, we were by nature deserving of wrath. But because of his great love for us, God, who is rich in mercy, made us alive with Christ even when we were dead in transgressions—it is by grace you have been saved. And God raised us up with Christ and seated us with him in the heavenly realms in Christ Jesus.

4. What has Jesus done for us that should compel us to live more trusting and surrendered lives?

Paul is not trying to get us to earn the blessing we have received by grace through Christ; but Paul is asking us to live in a way that shows we comprehend the WEIGHT of it.

5. What are specific and practical ways we can remember the greatness of grace and what Jesus has done for us so that we will be moved to grow in surrender?

....

....

....

....

6. What are some signs that we are not living with an awareness of God's grace? What gets in the way of us being grateful for the grace God lavishes on us?

....

....

....

....

> When we begin to understand all that God has done for us, is there any choice but to surrender?

PHILIPPIANS 4:11–13 NIV

I am not saying this because I am in need, for I have learned to be content whatever the circumstances. I know what it is to be in need, and I know what it is to have plenty. I have learned the secret of being content in any and every situation, whether well fed or hungry, whether living in plenty or in want. I can do all this through him who gives me strength.

7. How does contentment lead us toward a more surrendered life? What can we do to grow a heart and lifestyle of contentment in a world that encourages more and more and more?

Select volunteers to look up and read aloud the following passages to the group and discuss the questions:

Mark 10:17–31 and **Exodus 20:1–17**

8. Jesus was highlighting the incompleteness of the rich young ruler's surrender—what is Jesus highlighting in your life?

9. What is the thing that would make our surrender more full—in the same way the rich young ruler said "but I've done all of this" and Jesus highlighted that his surrender was still incomplete?

The secret to surrendering is NOT to try to do it alone, but to surrender everything to Jesus who gives you the strength.

Ephesians 4:22–24

10. As you grow in surrender, answer one of the questions below:

- What is one thing you need to "put off" and remove from your life? (you might want to look at Ephesians 4:22, 25–31)

....

....

....

- What is one thing you need to "put on" and develop in your life? (you might want to look at Ephesians 4:24, 28–29, 32)

....

....

....

We dress ourselves in our surrender
to God. Top to bottom.

—— CLOSING PRAYER ——

Spend time in your group praying in any of the following directions:

- Thank God for how he changes your character to be more like his when you surrender to him.

- Lift up praise for the amazing grace of God revealed in Jesus, and ask the Holy Spirit to help you live with a constant and growing awareness of this grace.

- Ask the Holy Spirit to give you power to "put off" the things that do not honor God and to "put on" those things that will grow your surrender to your Savior.

- Take a moment for silent prayer to confess the areas of sin and rebellion you are having a hard time "putting off." Ask God to soften your heart in this specific area.

OUR role is to choose surrender
and abide; to believe and trust he
is creating something in us and
through us that is more beautiful
than we could ever imagine.

Between-Sessions Personal Study

— 1. FRUITS OF THE SPIRIT CHRONICLE —

Over the next month, as you are consciously surrendering your life to God, keep a journal of ways you see God producing the fruits of the Spirit in your life as you are living more in step with the Spirit.

Galatians 5:22–23a NIV

> But the fruit of the Spirit is love, joy, peace, forbearance, kindness, goodness, faithfulness, gentleness and self-control.

Date: _____

How I observe my love for others changing:

....

....

....

(cont.)

A prayer of praise:

....
....
....

Date: _____

How I observe my joy or countenance changing:

....
....
....

A prayer of praise:

....
....
....

Date: _____

How I observe my ability to have peace changing:

....
....
....

A prayer of praise:

....
....
....

Date: _____

What fruit of the Spirit do I see manifesting in my life:

....
....
....

A prayer of praise:

....
....
....

Date: _____

What fruit of the Spirit do I see manifesting in my life:

....
....
....

A prayer of praise:

....
....
....

Date: _____

What fruit of the Spirit do I see manifesting in my life:

....
....
....

(cont.)

A prayer of praise:

....
....
....

Date: _____

What fruit of the Spirit do I see manifesting in my life:

....
....
....

A prayer of praise:

....
....
....

Date: _____

What fruit of the Spirit do I see manifesting in my life:

....
....
....

A prayer of praise:

....
....
....

Surrender is a letting go but not
for the sake of emptiness, but for
the sake of a greater fullness.

2. IDENTIFY THE OBSTACLES
TO SURRENDER

Begin this exercise by lifting up a simple but challenging prayer.

> Lord of grace and power,
> give me the courage and humility to look
> deep into my heart and identify where I
> am resisting full surrender to you.

Next, write down three specific areas of your life where you struggle surrendering the most, where putting off the old seems too difficult or foreign, and truly yielding your life to God's will feels more than a challenge:

• I find it difficult to surrender:

....

....

....

• I find it difficult to surrender:

....

....

....

• I find it difficult to surrender:

....

....

....

Prayerfully pick one of these areas and write out two or three specific requests from God to help you give this up or away or simply over. Ask God clearly for provision where you have not yet been able to surrender.

Finally, ask one or two close Christian friends to pray for you to receive God's help, encourage you to trust his provision, and keep you accountable as you take these steps and grow in surrender in this specific area.

Surrender requires trust.

— 3. CLEAN YOUR CLOSET —

Have you taken time to examine the contents of your closet lately? Looking at the various wardrobe pieces inside, you discover outfits you don't wear anymore, others that you can't fit into any longer, even clothes that are totally out of style. You realize it is time to clean the closet.

In this lesson we learned that one part of surrender is taking off old attitudes, behaviors, motives, and sinful patterns and throwing them out.

Over the next week, start to make a list of some things you still have in the closet of your life that should not be there. Use the prompts below to get you thinking. Write down what comes to your mind over the coming week.

My list of **motives** I should put off . . .

My list of **attitudes toward others** I should put off . . .

My list of **attitudes toward myself** I should put off . . .

My list of *behaviors* I should put off . . .

....

....

....

My list of *things I say* or ways I use my words that I should put off . . .

....

....

....

Other things I should put off . . .

....

....

....

Start with one of these areas and take steps to remove it while you put on something Christ-honoring in its place.

Who you are now is created after the very likeness of God. We don't just try hard to be newer, more surrendered people. We become new creations!

Keep a simple journal of what God is teaching you through these exercises and make special note of where you may need to simply surrender your ability to change, so that he can inspire transformation in you.

What changes when we surrender? Simply put, **we** change.

—— 4. REFLECT ——

Use the space provided below to write some reflections on the following topics:

- How is growing in trust and emptying myself leading to a fuller, more satisfying, joy-filled life?

....

....

- How is my trust in God and friendship with Jesus increasing as I surrender more?

....

....

- As I lay more and more of my life and myself on the altar in surrender to God, how am I becoming more content?

....

....

....

—— RECOMMENDED READING ——

As you reflect on what God is teaching you through this session, you may want to read chapter 10 of *I Give Up* by Laura Story. You also might want to read chapters 11–14 as you get ready for the next session.

The Ripple Effect of Surrender

— INTRODUCTION —

In the sixth chapter of the book of Galatians, Paul lays out how our motives can affect our results. What Paul is speaking about is similar to the Lord saying to Samuel that he looks at a person's heart, not his outward appearance (1 Samuel 16:7). Our motivation for surrender directly impacts the result of our surrender, on our lives as well as those around us. When we sow with self-serving motives, the results are often different than when we sow with purposeful and genuine motives for change:

Do not be deceived: God cannot be mocked. A man reaps what he sows. Whoever sows to please their flesh, from the flesh will reap destruction; whoever sows to please the Spirit, from the Spirit will reap eternal life. Let us not become weary in doing good, for at the proper time we will reap a harvest if we do not give up. Therefore, as we have opportunity, let us do good to all people, especially to those who belong to the family of believers.

GALATIANS 6:7–10 NIV

This concept is so true that most of us can predict what we will reap if we sow certain actions, attitudes, words, and behaviors. There are results that come to us, and those around us, when we do certain things.

Think about the cause and effects that we see in the flow of life. Read each of the lines below and give a few seconds of silence. Ask yourself, *What is the effect, what will be reaped, what are the certain results that will come from each of these scenarios?*

- He refuses to exercise or be physically active. He does not sleep much and always goes to bed after 1:00 AM. In addition, he eats only high sugar food, fast food, and he snacks until after midnight seven days a week. *What will this person and those around him reap as a result? Stop and reflect . . . paint a picture in your mind.*

- She is addicted to media and any kind of screen grabs her attention and won't let go. She binge-watches three to five hours of Netflix and Hulu every night. During the day, she is on her phone texting, updating her social media, or surfing a host of online sites she likes every moment she can. Most of the time she wears ear buds and can't hear what others are trying to say to her. Even in the middle of a conversation, she keeps checking her phone. *What will this person and those around her reap as a result? Stop and reflect . . . paint a picture in your mind.*

- He has a habit of pointing out the best in people and is quick to encourage those who are feeling down. He guards his tongue and strives to never gossip or pass on rumors about others. When he reads an encouraging article or tweet, he is quick to share it with others. When people are speaking poorly about someone who is not present he tends to remove himself from the situation or occasionally, with gentle thoughtfulness, suggests it is not wise to speak about that person if they are not there to defend themselves. *What will this person and those around him reap as a result? Stop and reflect . . . paint a picture in your mind.*

- She makes time each day, even in her busy schedule, to sit at the feet of Jesus and quietly listen to him speak through his Word and the still small voice of the Holy Spirit. When friends and even strangers tell her about a struggle they are facing, she offers to pray for them at that moment (when the setting allows) and she always prays in the coming days. She makes time to be in community with other Christians and seeks to offer grace, kindness, and service as she can. Jesus is her first priority and she plans her days with his will in mind. *What will this person and those around her reap as a result? Stop and reflect . . . paint a picture in your mind.*

Why can each of us immediately picture the results of each of these scenarios? Because every action, attitude, and thing we say has results. This is powerfully true when it comes to surrender. When you and I choose to live a surrendered life and declare "I give up," there are amazing results in us and every person around us.

People around us are blessed
by our surrender.

—— TALK ABOUT IT ——

Share what you expect to see in your life and the lives of the people around you as you seek to live truly surrendered to the will and ways of God.

or

What is one positive and encouraging thing that has happened in the last month in the life of someone close to you because you are living a more surrendered life to God?

Surrendering our lives to God has a ripple effect, from how we treat our mothers-in-law to how patient we are with the cable guy when we've been placed on hold for 30 minutes.

─── VIDEO TEACHING NOTES ───

As you watch the video teaching segment for this session, use the following outline to record anything that stands out to you.

None of us are perfect examples of surrender

....

....

....

....

When we surrender it impacts everyone around us

....

....

....

....

The story and example of Peter

....

....

....

Confidence in our ability to perform
a task isn't what God is looking
for. He is looking for dependence.
He is looking for willingness.

Surrender is unique to each of us

Why would God withhold something from us?

The presence and power of the Holy Spirit . . . a key to surrender

An Irish blessing

I give up!

Surrender is unique to each individual.
My surrender looks different than
your surrender. God may be calling
you to give up something that he
isn't calling your friend to give up.

— GROUP DISCUSSION —

Read each question and take time for group members
to give honest and thoughtful responses.

1. We all have areas of life where we lay something on the altar, seek to surrender, only to pick it up again and struggle to let go. What is one area of life where you face this dilemma? What step can you take toward giving this to God one more time and seeking to surrender?

2. We have been learning about surrender for five sessions. Tell about a step forward you have taken and how it has impacted (or will hopefully impact) others in your life. Or, tell about someone in your life who has actually noticed that you are growing in surrender and said something to you.

Select volunteers to read the following passages
aloud to the group and discuss the questions:

> **PHILIPPIANS 2:1–4** NIV
> Therefore if you have any encouragement from being united with
> Christ, if any comfort from his love, if any common sharing in the
> Spirit, if any tenderness and compassion, then make my joy complete
> by being like-minded, having the same love, being one in spirit and of
> one mind. Do nothing out of selfish ambition or vain conceit. Rather, in
> humility value others above yourselves, not looking to your own inter-
> ests but each of you to the interests of the others.

3. What from this passage do you learn about *Christ's* part in our journey of
   surrender? What from this passage do you learn about *our* part in living a
   surrendered life?

   ....

   ....

   ....

Surrender isn't some tactic we can use to
get God to finally relent and do it our way.

4. How have you been blessed by the life of a person who is truly surrendered to
   Jesus, and what life-patterns did they exhibit that led to a truly surrendered life?

   ....

   ....

   ....

JOHN 21:15–19 NIV

When they had finished eating, Jesus said to Simon Peter, "Simon son of John, do you love me more than these?" "Yes, Lord," he said, "you know that I love you."

Jesus said, "Feed my lambs." Again Jesus said, "Simon son of John, do you love me?"

He answered, "Yes, Lord, you know that I love you." Jesus said, "Take care of my sheep."

The third time he said to him, "Simon son of John, do you love me?"

Peter was hurt because Jesus asked him the third time, "Do you love me?" He said, "Lord, you know all things; you know that I love you."

Jesus said, "Feed my sheep. Very truly I tell you, when you were younger you dressed yourself and went where you wanted; but when you are old you will stretch out your hands, and someone else will dress you and lead you where you do not want to go." Jesus said this to indicate the kind of death by which Peter would glorify God. Then he said to him, "Follow me!"

5. What lessons is Jesus teaching Peter about surrender and what can we learn from Jesus' interaction with Peter?

How was Peter's call to surrender unique to who he was and what Jesus called him to do?

6. How did Jesus model surrender when he:

    •   Left heaven and came to live among us? (Matthew 2:1–2 and Philippians 2:6–7)

    •   Washed the disciples' feet? (John 13:1–17)

    •   Instituted communion by breaking the bread and pouring out the cup? (Matthew 26:17–30)

    •   Carried the cross and let himself be nailed to it for our sins? (John 19:17–18)

    •   Cried out, "My God, My God, why have you forsaken me?" (Matthew 27:45–46)

7. Each of us is called to surrender as we follow Jesus. What does your unique call to surrender look like and why is it important that we *not* try to follow someone else's pathway of surrender?

> If God is withholding something from you in this moment, it is for your good and for his greater glory. His timing is not ours and his ways are always higher.

8. Sometimes God withholds something from us for our own good and for his glory. Tell about a time God held something back and it was hard for you until you later realized that he was doing something bigger than you could recognize at first.

....

....

....

....

ACTS 1:12–14 NIV

Then the apostles returned to Jerusalem from the hill called the Mount of Olives, a Sabbath day's walk from the city. When they arrived, they went upstairs to the room where they were staying. Those present were Peter, John, James and Andrew; Philip and Thomas, Bartholomew and Matthew; James son of Alphaeus and Simon the Zealot, and Judas son of James. They all joined together constantly in prayer, along with the women and Mary the mother of Jesus, and with his brothers.

ACTS 2:14–16 NIV

Then Peter stood up with the Eleven, raised his voice and addressed the crowd: "Fellow Jews and all of you who live in Jerusalem, let me explain this to you; listen carefully to what I say. These people are not drunk, as you suppose. It's only nine in the morning! No, this is what was spoken by the prophet Joel . . .

9. Peter had denied Jesus three times, then ran away, and trembled and hid in the upper room. But he was filled with boldness and preached with power to those who had crucified Jesus. What happened to change Peter and lead him to a place of radical and courageous surrender (Acts 2:1–4)? What role does the Spirit of God have in our growth in surrender?

Peter couldn't see the scope of his surrender; none of us can. He was just asked to take the first step. He wasn't told the full story of how God would use his surrender; he was just asked to surrender.

10. What is your next big step toward living a surrendered life before Jesus, and how can your group members pray for you and cheer you on in this specific area of your spiritual journey?

—— CLOSING PRAYER ——

Spend time in your group praying in any of the following directions:

- Thank God for the people who have been (or are presently) examples of godly surrender in your life.

- Pray for a heart and life more like Jesus. Ask the Holy Spirit to make the example of Jesus a driving force in your journey toward deeper levels of surrender.

- Lift up one of your group members and pray for God to help them grow in the specific area of surrender that they long to see increased in their life.

- Invite the Holy Spirit to empower you with the perseverance it will take to live a lifetime of surrender beyond just this study. Pray that he would fill you with the full strength to endure and to continue to surrender even as things have not yet happened. Remember it is a life-long endeavor that God is committed to doing in us. Read aloud Philippians 1:6 NIV:

> Being confident of this, that he who began a good work in you will carry it on to completion until the day of Christ Jesus.

God is the only one who can see the full story, and our job is to trust him enough to surrender.

Final Personal Study

— 1. THANK YOU! —

Think and pray about someone who has given you a living picture of a surrendered life over many years. Write them a note thanking them for how God has used them to teach, inspire, and impact your life. If the person you think of is already with Jesus in glory, share this letter with their children or other family members.

> Living a surrendered life doesn't happen in a vacuum. And it's not just that people around us notice it; the people around us are blessed by it!

2. PREPARE FOR COMMUNION IN A NEW WAY

One of the ways Jesus taught us to surrender was through his humble and sacrificial death on the cross for our sins. When he instituted communion, he established a regular time for us to remember his sacrificial surrender and the price he paid for us.

When the hour came, Jesus and his apostles reclined at the table. And he said to them, "I have eagerly desired to eat this Passover with you before I suffer. For I tell you, I will not eat it again until it finds fulfillment in the kingdom of God."

After taking the cup, he gave thanks and said, "Take this and divide it among you. For I tell you I will not drink again from the fruit of the vine until the kingdom of God comes."

And he took bread, gave thanks and broke it, and gave it to them, saying, "This is my body given for you; do this in remembrance of me."

In the same way, after the supper he took the cup, saying, "This cup is the new covenant in my blood, which is poured out for you."

LUKE 22:14–20 NIV

Think through stories of Jesus in the Gospels and write down eight to ten things about Jesus' life and humble surrender that are important for you to remember. What did he do? How did he live and serve? Who did he love and lift up? Use the space provided to write down these memorable moments of surrender:

1.

2.

3.

4.

5.

6.

7.

8. ....

9. ....

10. ....

The next time you celebrate communion with God's people, read this list beforehand and meditate on all that Jesus surrendered for the people he loved. As you come to the table, carry these in your heart and celebrate Jesus with fresh eyes and renewed passion.

Time spent in God's Word and with God's people will affect not only our lives but every life around us.

—— 3. MY UNIQUE SURRENDER ——

The way we surrender is unique to each of us. Use the prompts below to gather some thoughts about ways you can become closer to whom God has made you to be. Think of all of the unique stories in the Bible—from Genesis to Revelation—of people who radically surrendered, each in his or her own way (Esther, Isaiah, Abraham, Mary, David, Paul, Peter, Solomon, Naomi, Jacob).

What are attitudes I carry in my heart that I need to surrender to God's will?

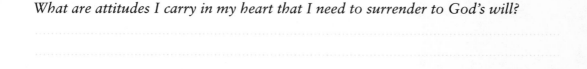

....

....

....

....

What are material things I hold too tightly that I need to surrender to God's care?

....

....

....

What are habits I engage in that I need to surrender to God's plan?

....

....

....

We're not suggesting that you go sew a flag and hang it on the front porch of your house (unless that is your thing), but do grab a piece of paper, write on it what you want to surrender, and post it on your mirror at home, on the dashboard of your car, on your computer at work—wherever you'll see it on a regular basis. It is just as important to acknowledge the day-to-day practice of surrender as the truths you learn.

May your surrender be both a great life change and a thousand little choices.

Keep a simple journal of what God is saying to you through the exercise over the past few weeks of study.

May we learn to say with joy, "I give up!"

—— 4. REFLECT ——

Use the space provided below to write some reflections on the following topics:

- How have these five sessions on surrender already changed my lifestyle, attitudes, and decisions?

- What area of stubborn resistance am I still not willing to surrender? Am I willing to ask God to give me power and a desire to surrender this behavior or attitude?

I surrender. I surrender. I choose to surrender.

—— RECOMMENDED READING ——

As you reflect on what God is teaching you through this session, you may want to read chapters 11–14 of *I Give Up* by Laura Story.

Small Group Leader Helps

If you are reading this, you have likely agreed to lead a group through *I Give Up*. Thank you! What you have chosen to do is important, and much good fruit can come from studies like this. The rewards of being a leader are different from those of participating, and we hope you find your own walk with Jesus deepened by this experience.

I Give Up is a five-session study built around video content and small-group interaction. As the group leader, imagine yourself as the host of a dinner party. Your job is to take care of your guests by managing all the behind-the-scenes details so that as your guests arrive, they can focus on each other and on interaction around the topic.

As the group leader, your role is not to answer all the questions or reteach the content—the video, book, and study guide will do most of that work. Your job is to guide the experience and cultivate your small group into a kind of teaching community. This will make it a place for members to process, question, and reflect—not receive more instruction.

There are several elements in this leader's guide that will help you as you structure your study and reflection time, so follow along and take advantage of each one.

BEFORE YOU BEGIN

Before your first meeting, make sure the participants have a copy of this study guide so they can follow along and have their answers written out ahead of time. Alternately, you can hand out the study guides at your first meeting and give the group members some time to look over the material and ask any preliminary questions. During your first meeting, be sure to send a sheet around the room and have the members write down their name, phone number, and email address so you can keep in touch with them during the week. Generally, the ideal size for a group is between eight to ten people, which ensures everyone will have enough time to participate in discussions. If you have more people, you might want to break up the main group into smaller subgroups. Encourage those who show up at the first meeting to commit to attending the duration of the study, as this will help the group members get to know each other, create stability for the group, and help you know how to prepare each week.

Each of the sessions begins with an opening illustration, which the leader can read or summarize. The choice of questions that follow serve as an icebreaker to get the group members thinking about the topic at hand. Some people may want to tell a long story in response to one of these questions, but the goal is to keep the answers brief. Ideally, you want everyone in the group to get a chance to answer, so try to keep the responses to a minute or less. If you have talkative group members, say up front that everyone needs to limit his or her answer to one minute.

Give the group members a chance to answer but tell them to feel free to pass if they wish. With the rest of the study, it's generally not a good idea to have everyone answer every question—a free-flowing discussion is more desirable. But with the opening icebreaker questions, you can go around the circle. Encourage shy people to share, but don't force them.

Before your first meeting, let the group members know that each session contains four days' worth of Bible study and reflection materials that they can complete during the week. While this is an optional exercise, it will help the members cement the concepts presented during the group study time and encourage them to spend time each day in God's Word. Also invite them to bring any questions and insights they uncovered while reading to your next meeting, especially if they had a breakthrough moment or if they didn't understand something.

WEEKLY PREPARATION

As the leader, there are a few things you should do to prepare for each meeting:

- *Read through the session.* This will help you to become familiar with the content and know how to structure the discussion times.

- *Decide which questions you definitely want to discuss.* Based on the amount and length of group discussion, you may not be able to get through all of the questions, so choose four to five questions that you definitely want to cover.

- *Be familiar with the questions you want to discuss.* When the group meets you'll be watching the clock, so you want to make sure you are familiar with the questions you have selected. In this way, you'll ensure you have the material more deeply in your mind than your group members.

- *Pray for your group.* Pray for your group members throughout the week and ask God to lead them as they study his Word.

- *Bring extra supplies to your meeting.* The members should bring their own pens for writing notes, but it's a good idea to have extras available for those who forget. You may also want to bring paper and additional Bibles.

Note that in many cases there will be no one "right" answer to the question. Answers will vary, especially when the group members are being asked to share their personal experiences.

—— STRUCTURING THE DISCUSSION TIME ——

You will need to determine with your group how long you want to meet each week so you can plan your time accordingly. Generally, most groups like to meet for either sixty minutes or ninety minutes, so you could use one of the following schedules:

Section	60 minutes	90 minutes
Introduction (members arrive and get settled; leader reads or summarizes introduction)	5 minutes	10 minutes
Talk About It (discuss one of the two opening questions for the session)	10 minutes	15 minutes
Video Notes (watch the teaching material together and take notes)	15 minutes	15 minutes
Group Discussion (discuss the Bible study questions you selected ahead of time)	25 minutes	40 minutes
Closing Prayer (pray together as a group and dismiss)	5 minutes	10 minutes

As the group leader, it is up to you to keep track of the time and keep things moving along according to your schedule. You might want to set a timer for each segment so both you and the group members know when your time is up. (Note that there are some good phone apps for timers that play a gentle chime or other pleasant sound instead of a disruptive noise.)

Don't be concerned if the group members are quiet or slow to share. People are often quiet when they are pulling together their ideas, and this might be a new experience for them. Just ask a question and let it hang in the air until someone shares. You can then say, "Thank you. What about others? What came to you when you watched that portion of the video?"

—— GROUP DYNAMICS ——

Leading a group through *I Give Up* will prove to be highly rewarding both to you and your group members. However, this doesn't mean you will not encounter any challenges along the way! Discussions can get off track. Group members may not be sensitive to the needs and ideas of others. Some might worry they will be expected to talk about matters that make them feel awkward. Others may express comments that result in disagreements. To help ease this strain on you and the group, consider the following ground rules:

- When someone raises a question or comment that is off the main topic, suggest you deal with it another time, or, if you feel led to go in that direction, let the group know you will be spending some time discussing it.

- If someone asks a question you don't know how to answer, admit it and move on. At your discretion, feel free to invite group members to comment on questions that call for personal experience.

- If you find one or two people are dominating the discussion time, direct a few questions to others in the group. Outside the main group time, ask the more dominating members to help you draw out the quieter ones. Work to make them a part of the solution instead of the problem.

- When a disagreement occurs, encourage the group members to process the matter in love. Encourage those on opposite sides to restate what they heard the other side say about the matter, and then invite each side to evaluate if that perception is accurate. Lead the group in examining other Scriptures related to the topic and look for common ground.

When any of these issues arise, encourage your group members to follow these words from the Bible: "Love one another" (John 13:34), "If it is possible, as far as it depends on you, live at peace with everyone" (Romans 12:18), and "Be quick to listen, slow to speak and slow to become angry" (James 1:19). This will make your group time more rewarding and beneficial for everyone who attends.

New from Laura Story

THE SECRET JOY OF A
SURRENDERED LIFE

I Give Up

AUTHOR OF WHEN GOD DOESN'T FIX IT

LAURA STORY
with Leigh McLeroy

Softcover
9780785226291

If you've enjoyed this Bible study, read more of Laura's journey of surrender in the companion book!

Newlywed Laura Story thought she had control over the great life ahead of her. After all, she followed Jesus and had a promising new job as a worship leader. Why would God not want to fulfill her dreams?

But when Laura and her husband, Martin, faced a brain tumor, infertility, and a son's birth defect, she realized she'd been looking for a happiness that comes from circumstances, rather than a deeper joy that comes from God. Again and again, Laura had to surrender her vision for her life so she could embrace God's vision. And again and again she learned that even in the midst of shattered dreams, God's plan brought greater joy than she could have imagined.

Available now at your favorite bookstore.

Also available: Laura's new album, *I Give Up* inspired by the secret of surrender.
Find it everywhere music is sold.

THOMAS NELSON
Since 1798

BIBLE STUDY SOURCE

for women

powered by ChurchSource

Connecting you with the best in

BIBLE STUDY RESOURCES

from many of the world's

MOST TRUSTED BIBLE TEACHERS

| LAURA STORY | MARGARET FEINBERG | ANN VOSKAMP | CHRISTINE CAINE |

Providing
WOMEN'S MINISTRY LEADERS,
SMALL GROUP LEADERS, AND INDIVIDUALS

with the
INSPIRATION, ENCOURAGEMENT, AND RESOURCES
every woman needs to grow their faith in every season of life

powered by ChurchSource

join our COMMUNITY

Use our BIBLE STUDY FINDER to quickly find the perfect study for your group,
learn more about all the new studies available, and download FREE printables
to help you make the most of your Bible study experience.

BibleStudySourceForWomen.com

FIND THE *perfect* BIBLE STUDY
for you and your group in 5 MINUTES or LESS!

Find the right study for your women's group
by answering four easy questions:

1. WHAT TYPE OF STUDY DO YOU WANT TO DO?

- *Book of the Bible:* Dive deep into the study of a Bible character, or go through a complete book of the Bible systematically, or add tools to your Bible study methods toolkit.

- *Topical Issues:* Have a need in a specific area of life? Study the Scriptures that pertain to that need. Topics include prayer, joy, purpose, balance, identity in Christ, and more.

2. WHAT LEVEL OF TIME COMMITMENT BETWEEN SESSIONS WOULD YOU LIKE?

- *None:* No personal homework
- *Minimal:* Less than 30 minutes of homework
- *Moderate:* 30 minutes to one hour of homework
- *Substantial:* An hour or more of homework

3. WHAT IS YOUR GROUP'S BIBLE KNOWLEDGE?

- *Beginner:* Group is comprised mostly of women who are new to the Bible or who don't feel confident in their Bible knowledge.

- *Intermediate:* Group has some experience with studying the Bible, and they have some familiarity with the stories in the Bible.

- *Advanced:* Group is comfortable with the Bible, and can handle the challenge of searching the Scriptures for themselves.

4. WHAT FORMAT DO YOU PREFER?

- *Print and Video:* Watch a Bible teacher on video, followed by a facilitated discussion.

- *Print Only:* Have the group leader give a short talk and lead a discussion of a study guide or a book.

Get Started! Plug your answers into the **Bible Study Finder**, and discover the studies that best fit your group!

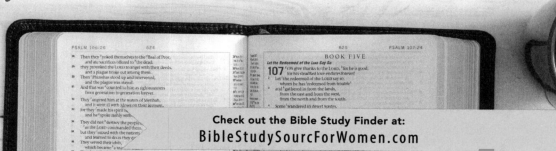

Check out the Bible Study Finder at:
BibleStudySourcForWomen.com

Also from Laura Story

In this five-session video Bible study, Laura examines the twists and turns that took place not only in her own life but also in the lives of many of the heroes of the faith. She reveals how God used crises in the lives of people such as Abraham, Sarah, David, and Paul to bring them closer to him and set them on the path he wanted them to take. She also shows how God used each of these individuals in spite of their flaws and brokenness.

God may not fix everything in our lives. In fact, our situation might not ever change or get better. But we can know that God will lead us to a place where we are better because of it.

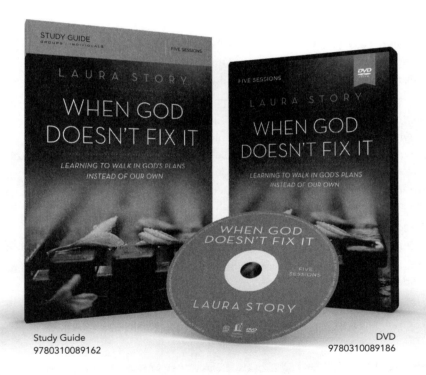

Study Guide
9780310089162

DVD
9780310089186

Available now at your favorite bookstore,
or streaming video on StudyGateway.com.